Contents

Getting Started

Introduction 2-3

Sewing glossary 4-5

Stitch guide 6-7

Tips 8

Beginner Projects

Bunting 9-11

Fabric Letters 12

Coin Purse 13-15

Hanging Hearts 16-17

Pin Cushion 18-19

Scrunchies 20

Notebook Cover 21

Fabric Coasters 22

Earphone Tidy 23

Simple Tote Bag 24-25

Intermediate Projects

Apron 26-27

Zipped Pouch 28-29

Needle Wrap 30-33

Thread Tidy 34-35

Sewing Caddy 36-38

Templates 39-47

DIY culture is on the rise, with more and more people taking up new hobbies and finding a sense of satisfaction and wellbeing in making things with their hands.

One of the oldest textile arts, sewing is an impressive, useful and incredibly rewarding skill to learn. With just a little practice, it's easy to make unique accessories and gifts.

This book will guide you through all the basics of sewing, from pressing and pinning to turning and topstitching (don't worry if you don't know what these terms mean – you soon will!). Consult the sewing glossary and stitch guide whenever you need to and follow the simple step-by-step instructions to create your own versions of the projects within.

There are 15 ideas included, complete with templates at the back that you can use again and again.

Start off with easy-peasy bunting or a coin purse and in no time, you'll be stitching compartments in a tool wrap and proudly modelling a handmade apron! All it takes is practice.

The projects are all designed with fat quarters in mind – once you've used up the fabrics included; you'll find lots more available in your local craft store.

Let's get Stitching

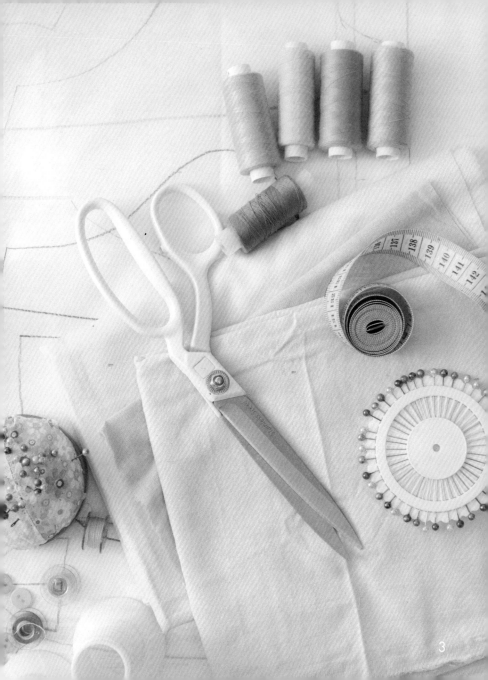

Sewing Glossary

Right side (RS) – The outside of a garment/project or front of a fabric.
Wrong side (WS) – The inside of a garment/project or back of a fabric.
Raw edge – The cut edge of your fabric before it has been hemmed or sewn.

Raw edges might fray if left unstitched, but a simple zigzag stitch will stop them unravelling.

Seam – The join where two or more layers of fabric are sewn together.
Seam allowance – The extra fabric between the edge and the stitching line.
Many patterns use a 1cm seam allowance, but you should always check carefully and follow the instructions given.
Press – Using an iron to press down into, rather than sliding across the fabric.
Used on seams, this important process gives garments shape.
Ease – To slightly gather a longer piece of fabric so it can be joined to a shorter one.
Clip the curve – Clip the curve/corners - After sewing a curved seam or corner, instructions will often ask you to 'clip the curve' or 'clip the corners'. This simply means that before you turn the project right side out, you'll need to cut small notches out of the seam allowance to reduce the bulk of the fabric. When clipping a curve on the outer edge, use straight cuts.

Use small notches when clipping the curve to reduce the fabric bulk.

Fusible interfacing/fleece – Sew-in or iron-on fabric used to shape, add body or reinforce foundation fabrics.

Double thread – Doubling your thread over gives you a slightly stronger thread to work with. Thread it through the eye of the needle and pull through until both ends are the same length. Knot the ends together to secure.

Bias binding – A cut strip used to bind or cover edges. Slightly stretchy, it sews neatly around curves.

Patchwork – The technique of sewing pieces of fabric together to create a larger piece of fabric.

Appliqué – A decorative technique of cutting out then sewing or fusing small pieces of fabric onto a foundation piece.

Quilting – The technique of sewing together two layers of fabric with a wadding material in the middle to create a thicker, padded piece.

Bodkin – A tool that helps replace drawstrings or thread through a channel. It looks like an oversized needle with a large eye and a blunt point. If you don't have a bodkin, you can use a safety pin instead.

Before You Start

For every project in this book, you'll need the following essentials. Additional materials are noted on the relevant page.

- Sewing machine (or a needle if you prefer to hand-sew)
- Fabric fat quarters (cotton works best)
- Threads in colours to match your fabrics
- Scissors
- Pins
- Iron

Stitch Guide

For all these projects, we recommend using a sewing machine. There are lots of sewing machines on the market, ranging from basic, entry-level machines to all-singing, all-dancing ones with LCD screens. You don't need anything too fancy to make the projects in this book; a simple machine will be perfect. Refer to your manufacturer's instructions to set up and thread your machine. There's no reason why you can't attempt to sew the projects by hand – it might just take a little longer!
Consult the stitch guide below to experiment with different styles.

Running stitch – The most widely used stitch for sewing simple hems and two pieces of fabric together, running stitch is created by weaving the needle in and out of the fabric.

Backstitch – Simply put, backstitch is sewing backwards. When using a machine, backstitch is used instead of a knot at the start and end to secure stitches and stop them unravelling.

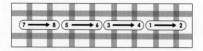

Topstitch – A topstitch is any stitch you sew on top of the fabric. It is usually decorative, sewn parallel to or along a hem on the right side of the fabric, or it may be used to add detail and shape to a design. In many cases the stitch is functional too, anchoring seam allowances in place and reinforcing the seams. Topstitching will give your finished projects a real quality look.

When practicing topstitching, use a slightly longer stitch length and use a thread that matches the fabric until you are confident in sewing straight lines. Press when finished to set and remove any puckering.

Edgestitch – An edgestitch is sewn very close to the fabric edge, giving a nice, crisp edge with a tailored look.

Zigzag stitch – For knit or stretchy fabric, a zigzag stitch is perfect as the stitches themselves can stretch with the fabric. It is also used to sew along a raw edge to help prevent the fabric from fraying.

∧∧∧∧∧∧∧∧∧∧∧∧∧∧∧

Ladder stitch – When a project has to be turned right side out at the last minute, you'll need to leave a small gap for turning and sew it closed by hand. A ladder stitch is used here to make sure the stitches remain unseen. Pin your folded sides together, draw a knotted thread up through a folded crease and put a small stitch in the opposite folded crease. Keep alternating all the way along the opening.

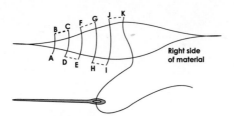

Slipstitch – A slipstitch is another easy way to sew a seam from the outside of the garment, by hand, and make sure it is invisible. Start inside your hem, hiding your knot in the fold. Catch just a few threads from the main fabric and run your needle back through the fold near your previous stitch. Again, take a few threads from the main fabric and run through the fold. Repeat along the seam.

Basting – To baste means to sew long, loose running stitches to temporarily hold fabric in place. This stitch is an alternative to pins, and is removed once a permanent seam has been made.

Top Tips

- Get everything ready before you start. Have pins and scissors to hand, and set up your iron ready to press your fabric as you go. Match threads to your fabric before you begin. Being prepared will mean you won't have to stop and hunt around for things mid-project!

- Try out your machine stitches on a scrap piece of fabric first, and adjust the settings accordingly until the stitch is your desired length and width.

- If you find your stitches become too tight or loose while sewing, rethread your machine, including the bobbin. 9 times out of 10, this will solve the problem!

- Always secure your stitching by backstitching at the beginning and end. Once you've sewn a few stitches, press reverse on your machine and go backwards before continuing forwards.

- To create nice, straight seams, don't look at your needle as you sew! Instead, measure your seam allowance using the needle plate.

- Control your speed! As a beginner it's best to take it as slowly as you can to avoid mistakes. Try operating the pedal with your bare foot – this will give you much better control than with shoes on.

- Remember to remove any pins as you sew.

- When sewing corners or when you need to move the fabric slightly, make sure you stop sewing with the needle in the fabric. Pivoting with the needle still in the fabric will help you achieve a perfectly aligned seam.

- Press your seams as you go. Well pressed seams will make a huge difference to the finished project! Press each seam before another crosses through it.

- When adding fusible interfacing to your fabric, use a cool iron and turn off the steam. Do not let your iron touch the fusible side.

Bunting

Bunting is a must-have decoration for a party or celebration. It's easily customised; try festive fabrics for Christmas, orange and black for Halloween or delicate florals for a summer garden party. Bunting isn't restricted to special occasions though; pretty flags bring a distinctive, handmade and homely feel to any room. You can buy fat quarters in stacks of coordinating colours and complementary styles, making it easy to whip up the perfect design in a flash.

Bunting is a fantastic beginner's project, as it only requires basic sewing know-how but will also introduce you to some key techniques. Select your fabric and let's get started!

1. Enlarge the templates so they are the size you want. We enlarged them by 200%. Cut them out and use them to cut pairs of flags from your chosen fabric.

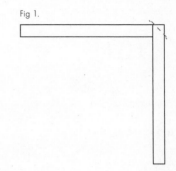

Fig 1.

2. Place the flags RS to RS and pin together. Sew around the edge of each flag leaving a 5mm seam allowance. Leave the top of the flags unsewn. Clip the bottom corners of the seams at the points of the bunting to reduce the bulk of fabric.

3. Turn the flags to the right side pushing the corners out firmly with a blunt pencil or similar. Press and then trim the tops of the flags with a rotary cutter to be sure they are straight.

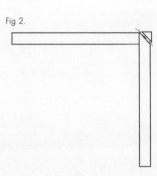

Fig 2.

4. To make the binding, cut 5cm strips of coordinating fabric. Place ends of two strips RS together at right angles to one another. Pin and then sew across the corner to join the strips. (fig. 1) Repeat until your binding is as long as you would like. Open the strips and press flat. Cut off the excess corner fabric. (fig. 2)

5. Fold the strip in half lengthwise (along line '1') and press. Unfold and then fold and press the two outer edges to the centre point (along lines '2'). Fold the whole strip in half (along line '1') and press again. (fig. 3)

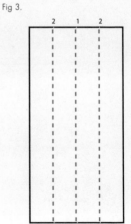

Fig 3.

6. Insert the top edge of the flags into the open edge of the binding, spacing them at regular intervals. Pin in place and then top stitch along the bottom edge of the binding tucking the very ends of the strip in, to secure the flags in place. Add a second row of stitching to finish.

Fabric Letters

Extra supplies needed:

- Batting
- Pinking Shears
- Fine Pointed Scissors

Spell out a special name or word for a cute decoration or make a whole alphabet to make learning fun!

1. Draw or print letters onto thin paper to your chosen size.

2. Cut two pieces of fabric and one piece of batting larger than each of your letters. Arrange with the fabric either side of the batting right sides facing out.

3. Pin the paper templates on top and sew along the lines of the letters using a straight stitch. Gently tear away the paper template.

4. Using pinking shears to cut close to the stitching. Use fine pointed scissors to cut the centres from the letters.

Coin Purse

Extra supplies needed:

- Fusible interfacing
- 9cm purse clasp with holes

This simple yet sweet project uses two layers of fabric – outer and lining – with a layer of fusible interfacing to give it shape. Choose two contrasting fabrics for the inner and outer and get started; you'll be amazed at how quickly this purse comes to life!

1. Cut out 1 x outer fabric, 1 x lining fabric and 1 x interfacing using the template on page 43.

2. Lay interfacing with (shiny) glue side up and place the outer fabric on top right side up. Using a medium iron and a cloth press the layers together. Hold the iron down for 5-10 seconds. Check the layers are fused together, if not, press again holding the iron in place a little longer.

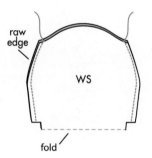

3. Fold the outer fabric with right sides facing. Sew down both sides 5mm from the raw edge.

4. Flatten the base and fold down the side seam so that the raw edges are lined up.

5. Sew along the raw edge. Do this for both sides.

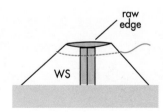

6. Repeat step 2 for the lining fabric.

7. Turn the outer fabric right side out and place inside the lining (still wrong side out). Match up the top edges. Sew around the top leaving a 4cm gap at the top of one of the upper most curves for turning.

8. Pull the whole purse through the gap. Flatten out and press, making sure the gap is pressed back into a curve. Top stitch close to the top edge all the way around. This will close the gap and neaten the edge so the layers won't move about when you hand sew.

9. Insert the top of the purse up inside the clasp, starting at the top centre. Baste with stitches going over the frame to help hold in place.

10. Using doubled up thread, sew the fabric in place using a running stitch through the holes in one side of the clasp. Going from the back to the front can be a little tricky, you must ensure you catch the fabric. When you get to the end of one side go back on yourself. Secure by stitching a few stitches in place. Repeat on the other side of the clasp. Remove basting stitches.

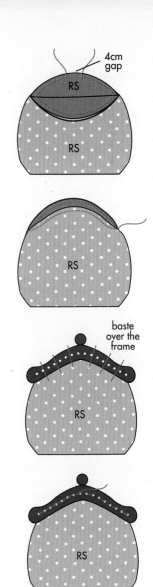

Hanging Hearts

Extra supplies needed:

- Ribbon
- Embellishments such as seed beads or sequins (optional)
- Toy stuffing

These cute little hearts are perfect for practicing curved corners, and you can add decorative elements to your heart's content to make each one as individual as the last. Once you've got the basics, why not try appliquéing or embroidering extra detail?

Hang in the window or on a door knob to add charm to your home, or fill with herbs and place in your drawers to keep sheets and towels smelling sweet.

1. Using the larger heart template on pages 39 and 40, cut out two hearts from your fabric.

2. Now is the time to add decoration if you wish. For a simple idea to start with, cut out two more fabric hearts using the smaller heart templates. With both fabric pieces facing right side up, pin and zigzag stitch the smaller heart on to the larger one, then add the smallest. You could also add embroidered detail, seed beads or sequins to embellish your decoration.

3. Measure out and cut 20cm of ribbon. Fold in half and position on the top centre of one of the heart pieces, matching the raw edges. Loosely baste into position.

4. Place the heart pieces together, right sides facing. Pin together, ensuring your ribbon is tucked inside but won't get caught up in the sewing machine.

5. Sew around the heart, 5mm from the edge. Backstitch over the ribbon to ensure it is fully secured. Leave a 3cm gap along one of the straight sides unsewn.

6. Clip the curves along the top of the heart to reduce the excess fabric there. Snip a deep 'V' at the top.

7. Pull the heart right side out through the 3cm gap at the side. Use a pencil or chopstick to push the curves and point out fully and press.

8. Fill your heart with small pieces of toy stuffing and hand-stitch the gap closed using a ladder stitch.

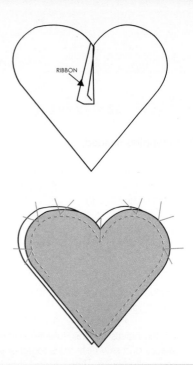

RIBBON

Pin Cushion

Extra supplies needed:

- Stuffing
- 2 x buttons – we used fabric covered buttons.
- Embroidery thread

Every crafter needs a pin cushion, and this lovely design will make a very stylish home for all your pins! A simple embroidery technique turns this simple make into an eye-catching wonder.

1. Iron your fabric and cut out the templates from pages 42 and 43.

2. For the pincushion top, take two of the triangular pieces and sew right sides together with a 0.5cm seam allowance. Then sew another piece on either side to form a semi-circle. Trim any excess fabric from the centre of the semi-circle. Repeat to make a second semi-circle. Press your seams open and sew both semi-circles together. Don't worry too much if you have a slight gap as this will be covered with a button later.

3. Pin the two circles together right sides facing.

4. Using a sewing machine, sew around the circle using a 1cm seam allowance and leave a gap large enough to allow you to stuff the cushion. Mark the gap with tailor's chalk to remind you not to stitch all the way around. Once sewn, clip the circle edges inwards to create ease around the seam. Be careful not to clip too close to the stitching.

Why not try...

At step 3, add a tab label into the seam for an extra finishing touch.
Fold the label in half, right sides facing in and sew along the side edges. Turn right sides out and place inside the seam of the pin cushion, central to 1 of the patchwork segments and the label sitting inside the circle. Check positioning, making sure the raw edges are together.

Create your own fabric covered buttons:
Cut out the small circle templates on page 42.
Use a running stitch around the edge of the circle, leaving a long tail of thread at the start and end of your stitching.
Place the fabric face down on your work surface. Add your button upside down in the centre and pull the threads to gather the fabric around the button.
Tie a couple of knots to secure in place. You can cover any buttons in this way – but for best results use smooth round buttons with a shank.

5. Turn right side out and stuff your pin cushion. Hand stitch up the gap with ladder stitch.

6. Thread your embroidery needle with the embroidery thread. This thicker thread is suitable for heavier stitching – there is no need to separate the strands for this project.

7. Pass your threaded needle down through the centre of the pin cushion, then bring the thread up on the outside, along the edge of one segment, and take it back through the centre. Pull the stitch tight enough to keep it in place and create a tucked in shape. Repeat until you have divided all the segments around the cushion.

8. Tie off your thread by stitching it into the centre of the bottom of your pin cushion. You can then tack the thread into place along the segment lines using a normal needle and thread to prevent movement slipping.

9. Sew a button in the centre of both the top and bottom of your pin cushion.

Scrunchies

Extra supplies needed:

- 0.5cm or 1cm elastic
- Safety Pins

Scrunchies are quick and easy to make – they'd make a great gift.

1. Cut fabric to measure 45cm by 12cm. Fold over one short end and top stitch to make a finished edge.

2. Fold the fabric in half lengthwise with wrong side together to make a tube. Sew along the length with a 0.5cm seam, leaving the ends open. Turn to the right side.

3. Cut elastic to measure 16cm. Thread through the tube securing the end with a safety pin and using another to feed the elastic through. Knot or stitch the ends together.

4. Insert the raw end of the tube into the finished end. Stitch across the finished end to close the scrunchie.

Notebook Cover

Extra supplies needed:

· Tape Measure
· Notebook

Make an ordinary notebook extraordinary with a quick and easy to make cover in your favourite fabric! Just adjust the sizing to suit any notebook or diary.

1. Measure your notebook from top to bottom and add 3cm.

2. Measure the whole length of the cover, including both covers and the spine. Add approximately 13cm.

3. Cut two pieces of fabric to the dimensions calculated above.

4. Place the two pieces with right sides together and stitch with a 0.5mm seam allowance leaving a 3cm gap on one short edge. Turn to the right side and push the corners out fully.

5. Top stitch close to both short edges.

6. Wrap the cover around your notebook, folding the excess length inside the notebook covers, and adjust until the fabric cover is snug with the edges lined up neatly. Pin in place and remove the cover from the book.

7. Top stitch around the edge of the cover with a 0.25cm seam allowance. Press and place onto your notebook.

21

Fabric Coasters

Extra supplies needed:

- Batting
- Pinking shears

A set of fabric coasters make a cute gift – Start with square for the easiest to make or try circular for a bit more of a challenge! This project is great for using up your scraps.

1. Cut several strips of fabric and join together with narrow seams. Press.

2. Cut the pieced section to a circle (or whatever shape you prefer) using pinking shears to around 11-12cm cutting a second shape to match from a coordinating fabric. Cut batting to measure 1.5cm smaller.

3. Place fabric with wrong sides together and sew with a 0.5cm seam allowance leaving a 3cm gap unsewn. Turn to right side and press.

4. Insert the batting through the hole and smooth out. Turn the edges of the unsewn section inside and pin. Top stitch around the perimeter of the coaster.

5. Quilt the coaster by sewing along the joins of the fabric strips.

Earphone Tidy

Extra supplies needed:

- Button
- Buttonhole foot for your machine

Keeping your cables and headphones untangled in your bag of pocket seems like an impossible task, but with this quick project it's no longer a problem!

1. Cut fabric to measure 12x12 cm. Fold in half with right sides together and stitch around the three open edges leaving a 3cm gap open with a 0.5cm seam allowance.

2. Turn to the right side, tuck the seam allowance at the gap in and press.

3. Top stitch around the whole rectangle near to the edge of the piece.

4. Follow the instructions on your sewing machine to sew a button hole to fit your button towards one end of the rectangle.

5. If you do not have a sewing machine cut a small slit in the fabric. Use a tight blanket stitch around the slit. Use a second layer of blanket stitch if necessary.

6. Stitch a button towards the other end of the rectangle.

Blanket Stitch

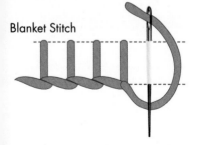

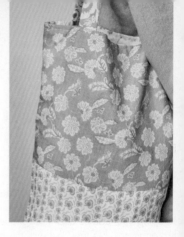

Simple Tote Bag

Ditching the plastic in favour of a reusable bag is definitely the environmentally friendly choice and this simple how-to will let you make your own! You'll be even more likely to remember it too when it's using your favourite fabric!

Fig 1.

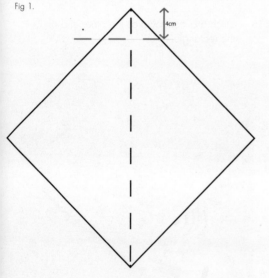

4cm

1. Cut 4 pieces of coordinating fabric each measuring 22cm x 55cm. Stitch pairs of the pieces together to make two larger panels. These will make your bag outer and lining.

2. Fold each panel in half with right sides together. Stitch along the long edge and one short edge.

3. To 'box' the corners, pinch the bottom corners of each piece, lining up the side seam (or fold) with the bottom seam. Measure in 4cm from the point and draw a line at right angles. Stitch along this line and trim off the excess. (fig.1)

4. Place the bag sections inside one another with right sides together.

Making the handles

5. Cut two pieces to measure 55cm x 12cm. Fold each piece in half with wrong sides together and press. Open and fold each edge into the centre. Press and then fold in half to make a 3cm wide strip. Top stitch along the open edge.

6. Position the handles between the lining and the outer layer with the handle ends lined up with the raw edge of the bag. Stitch around leaving an 8cm gap. (fig.2)

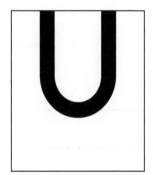

Fig 2.

7. Turn the bag to the right side, pushing the liner inside. Top stitch around the top of the bag.

Apron

Extra supplies needed:

- Bias binding
- Bodkin

Every crafter needs an apron, and now you've got all the know-how, you may as well look the part! This chic apron has a compartmentalised pocket to hold all your stitching necessities, from measuring tape and tailor's chalk to pins and spare thread. No matter where you are, everything you need will be to hand.

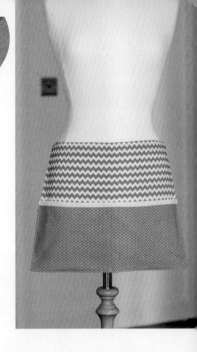

1. Cut out all the fabric pieces using the templates on page 46.

2. Fold the pocket piece in half lengthways, wrong sides together, pin and press.

3. Cut a piece of bias tape the length of your pocket panel. Fold the tape lengthways, but not quite in half, so one side is around 2mm longer. Press.

4. Open out the bias tape and pin the shorter side, right side facing, to the folded, closed edge of the pocket. Sew along the length of the first crease.

5. Fold the other side of the bias tape over, sandwiching the folded pocket edge inside. Pin, press and topstitch over the seam line between the tape and fabric, catching the 2mm overhang on the back.

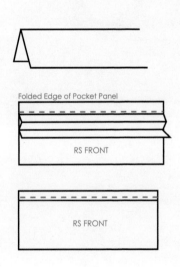

Folded Edge of Pocket Panel

RS FRONT

RS FRONT

. Position, pin and baste the pocket on top of one of the apron pieces, right side facing up. All raw edges should be aligned along the bottom and sides of the apron piece.

. Place the other apron layer on top, right side down, and pin all layers together.

. Sew along the top of the apron, 1cm from the edge. Sew the sides, leaving a 3cm gap each side for the straps. Sew along the bottom, leaving a gap of about 10cm for turning.

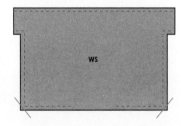

. Clip the corners at the bottom, getting rid of the excess fabric, and turn the apron out through the gap. Make sure the seams are pushed out fully, and the seam allowances in the gaps are folded in. Close the 10cm gap using ladder or slipstitch and press.

0. Topstitch 3mm from the top edge of the apron. Topstitch down the sides, again leaving a 3cm gap each side for the straps. Topstitch along the bottom. This will secure your pocket in place.

1. To create a channel for your strap, topstitch another line 3.5cm from the top edge.

12. Measure along the length of the pocket to find the centre and topstitch a line from the bottom up to the top of the bias tape. This will give you a handy divide in your pocket.

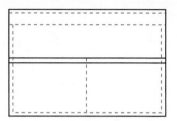

13. Place the two strap pieces right sides together and sew one short end 1cm from the edge to create one long strap. Press the seam open. Fold in half along the length, wrong sides together, and press again.

14. Fold one edge in 1cm and press and repeat with the other side. Open out the ends, fold in 1cm, press, refold and pin. Your strap should now measure 2.5cm wide.

15. Topstitch 2-3mm from the edge, all the way round the strap.

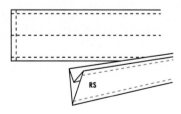

16. Use a large bodkin (or a safety pin, if you don't have a bodkin) to thread the strap through the channel.

Zipped Case

Extra supplies needed:

- Zip
- Zip foot for your sewing machine.

You can make these handy pouches in any size to suit any purpose. You're only limited by the size of your zip.

> Adjust the measurements to suit your chosen pouch size. You can make pouches much smaller than your zip if you need to as you'll be trimming off the excess!

1. To make a pouch measuring 10cm by 18cm (a great size for a pencil case or for glasses) cut two contrasting fabric pieces each measuring 36cm by 12cm. Line the short end of the outer piece with the edge of the zip with right sides together (use the middle of zip). Line the lining piece up with the wrong side of the zip. Pin in place and sew close to the zip using a zip foot. You may find it helpful when you get to the zip pull, to lift the presser foot with the needle in the fabric to enable you to slide the zip pull along out of the way.

2. Pin the other ends of the fabric pieces onto the other edge of the zip as before. Sew close to the zip.

3. Open the zip pull and carefully top stitch close to the fabric either side of the zip.

4. Turn to the wrong side, positioning the zip towards the top of the pouch and making sure the zip pull is positioned within the size of the pouch, but also open slightly.

5. Sew along the length of the pouch straight across the zip and going back and forth across the teeth a couple of times.

6. Use pinking shears to cut close to the seam trimming off the excess fabric and zip.

7. Turn to the right side through the zip and press.

Tip: A zip foot lets you sew much closer to the teeth of the zip than a regular foot.
Follow your sewing machine manufacturer's instructions.

Needle Wrap

Extra supplies needed:

- Fusible fleece
- Tailor's chalk
- Bias binding

If you're ready to go one step further with your new sewing skills, this needle wrap is the perfect challenge. It may look impressive, but by following the simple instructions below you'll be surprised how easily you can create your own. The wrap looks great with contrasting fabrics used for the outside and inside. Learn how to use bias binding on a more complex level than seen on the bunting on pages 9 and 11 and discover how to use simple stitched lines to create mini compartments to keep all your tools neat.

What's more, this handy organiser rolls up and ties together (another great use of bias binding!) so you can take your sewing stash with you everywhere you go.

1. Cut out your fabric pieces using the templates on pages 44 and 45. As this pattern has slightly more pieces than the others you've done so far, it's a good idea to label them all so you don't get them mixed up.

2. Cut another outer piece from fusible fleece. Lay the fusible fleece with the adhesive side up and place your outer panel piece on top, wrong side down. Press gently with an iron on medium heat until the fabrics have fused together.

3. The fleece will sit inside the fabrics to give the needle wrap the padded effect seen in quilted items. Flip your fused piece over and place the inner panel on top, wrong side down. Pin all three layers together to create a base piece.

4. Pin the small pocket front and small pocket lining together right sides facing. Sew lengthways along one side only, approximately 1cm from the raw edge.

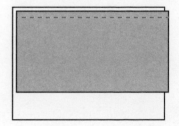

5. Repeat step 4 with the large pocket front and lining. Press the seams open on both pockets. Fold the pockets wrong side facing and match the two long edges. Press. Topstitch along the seams, using a decorative stitch such as zigzag.

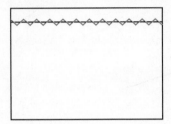

6. Take the flap piece and fold in half lengthways. Press the fold. Topstitch 2cm from the fold with a decorative stitch as you did with the pockets.

7. Lay the base piece in front of you, with the inner fabric facing up. Position and pin the flap piece at the top, aligning all the fabric edges.

8. Pin the large pocket on top of the base piece, aligning with the bottom edges and sides. Pin the small pocket on top of the large pocket, again aligning with the bottom edge and sides. Baste through all layers, securing everything into place. Use scissors to round off the corners.

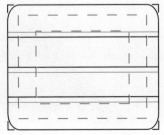

9. Determine the centre of the base piece. Draw the centre quilt line of the compartments with tailor's chalk (you can use pencil if you don't have tailor's chalk). Draw lines either side of the centre line, at 2.5cm intervals, to the edge of the wrap.

10. Sew over each of the lines you've drawn, starting in the centre and topstitching each marked line. Don't be tempted to turn the fabric and sew – each line must be sewn in the same direction. Keep an eye on the fabric to make sure it hasn't shifted. Make sure all sides are straight and even, and trim if necessary.

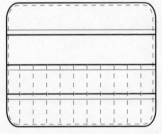

11. Now your compartments are complete, you need to add the bias binding around the edge. You may find it easier to edgestitch all around the outside of the panel and remove the basting stitches before you do so.

12. Measure your project, and cut the bias binding an inch or so longer than you need. Fold and press the tape lengthways. Cut one end at a 45-degree angle and fold the raw edge inside 0.5cm. Press. Because you have rounded the corners, you

can simply ease the tape round the wrap - open it out and pin to the edge of your fabric, on the inner side.

13. Sew along the first crease line, then fold the tape over, enclosing the fabric edge. By hand, use slipstitch to attach the bias binding all around the outer edge. Overlap the ends when they meet, trim the excess and backstitch to secure.

14. Take another length of bias binding and fold it in half lengthways. Press. Fold each end inside 1cm, press again, then sew down the length to create a tie for your wrap. Find the centre and hand-stitch securely to the centre of the outside of the wrap.

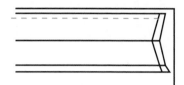

Thread Tidy and Pin Cushion
– A sewing essential.

Extra supplies needed:

- Stuffing

An essential project for any keen crafter – keep all those thread and fabric scraps tidy and your needles conveniently to hand while you work!

(This make uses 2 fat quarters – labelled A and B below)

Tip: You can amend the length of the connecting piece depending how low you wish your bag to hang below your table – or simply tuck a little away and secure with a safety pin underneath the weighted section so it is adjustable!

1. To make the bucket section, from fabric A cut one piece, 41cm x 24cm for the outer. Repeat for fabric B for the lining. Fold in half to make a tube measuring 20.5cm by 24cm with right sides together. Hem along the long edge and one short edge with a 0.5cm seam allowance.

2. Move the side seam to the centre of the tube and fold the corners to points. Measure 3cm along the centre seam of each point and stitch at right angles across the point only. Cut off the excess from each corner. Repeat steps 1 and 2 with the lining piece.

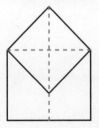
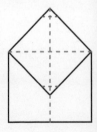

3. To make the connecting piece, cut two pieces of fabric B to measure 8cm x 14cm. Place RS together and stitch along both long edges. Turn to the right side and press. Top stitch along both long edges.

4. Cut 1 piece from fabric A to measure 13cm x 18cm. Fold in half with right sides together. Insert the connecting piece inside lining up the raw edges with the long edge (you will need to fold the connecting piece so that it fits inside). Hem around with a 0.5cm seam allowance, leaving one side open. Turn to the right side and press.

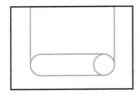

5. Turn the lining part of the bucket section so the right side is facing out. Place inside the outer part so right sides are facing together and line up the seams on one side. Insert the connecting piece between the two bucket pieces with the piece positioned at the back of the bucket and lining up the raw edges.

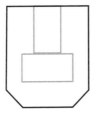

6. Sew around the top edge of the bucket piece with a 1cm seam allowance and leaving 7cm gap to turn. Turn to the right side and press. Top stitch around the bucket.

7. The last job is to fill your pin cushion. You might like to use sand or uncooked rice. I chose to use a metal plate from the hardware store with fibrefill on top for the pincushion.

> **Tip:** You can fill the weighted pin cushion section with all sorts of things you have to hand! Sand is great as it can help to keep your needles sharp, but uncooked rice can work also.

Sewing Caddy

Extra supplies needed:

· Fusible interfacing

This nifty little sewing basket is neat enough to sit on your desk or move around with you to wherever you're working, but it's still plenty roomy enough to hold all your stash essentials. Fill it up with your pin cushion (see pages 18 and 19!), cotton spools and all the other knick-knacks currently cluttering up your workspace.

1. Cut out the templates on page 47 and cut 2 pieces of interfacing 30 x 44cm.

2. Iron interfacing onto the wrong side of the 2 large fabric pieces and place wrong sides together. Decide which side you want as your inner basket fabric and place face down.

3. Pin the smaller pieces together wrong sides facing. Determine which fabric you want as the pocket lining and place face down.

4. Fold and press the bias tape with one side slightly lower than the other. Open the tape up and pin to the edge of your fabric. Sew along the first fold line. Fold the bias tape over, enclosing the fabric. From the front, pin along the 'ditch' (the first line of stitching) being sure to catch the tape on the back. Stitch in the ditch.

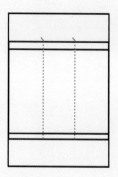

5. Pin or baste the pocket piece to the main piece, ensuring it is centered.

6. Mark 10cm from both edges of the bindings and sew a straight line from the top edge of the top binding to the bottom edge of the bottom binding - as shown below.

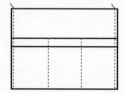

7. Fold in half wrong sides facing.

8. Sew close to the edge on both sides. Trim and turn inside out. Sew down the sides again to enclose the raw edge. Turn right side out.

9. Open out and flatten the side seams. Mark a 10cm line with the seam at the centre. Sew and trim excess corner close to the stitching. Turn inside out and sew along the same edge. Repeat for both ends - as shown below.

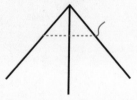

10. Press creases from the corners to the top of the basket and also press a crease between the corners front and back

11. Fold over the top edge 2cm, press and fold over again 2cm. Open out the fold and cut away some bulk by trimming the inner fabric down to the first crease line.

Snip away some of the bulk at the side seams. Fold back over and pin in place - as shown below.

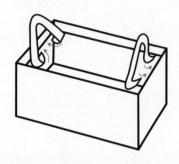

12. Fold 2 x 25cm of bias binding in half and sew along the edge to create the handles. Insert the ends of the handles under the fold close to the corners. Fold up and pin in place - as shown below.

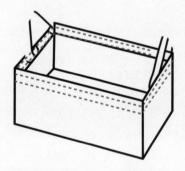

13. Top stitch around the top edge 1.5cm from the top. Top stitch again 0.5cm from the top edge. You may need to turn the needle by hand over the seams. Mark 10cm from both edges of the bindings and sew a straight line from the top edge of the top binding to the bottom edge of the bottom binding.

Templates

Where templates need to be enlarged, use a scanner and printer or photocopier, and set to the percentage given.

Hanging hearts

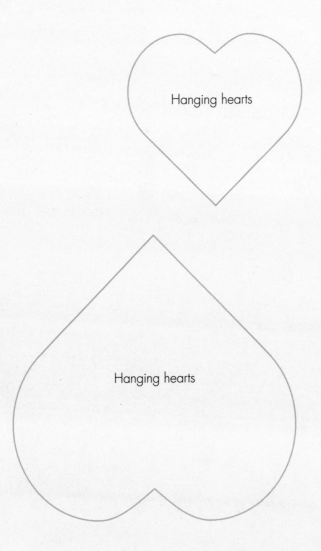

Hanging hearts

Hanging hearts

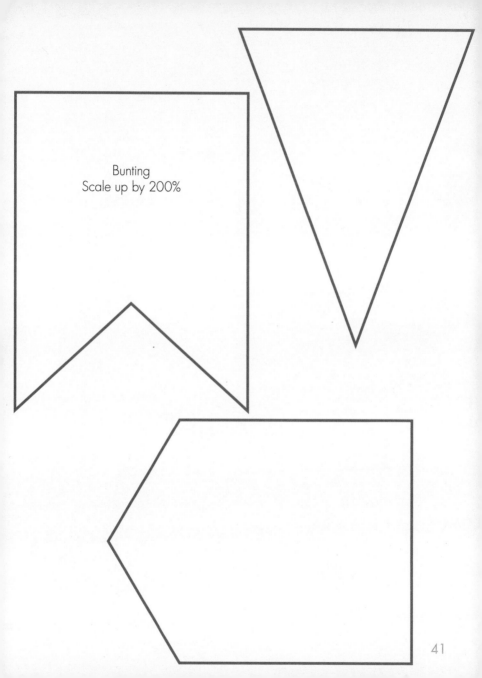

Bunting
Scale up by 200%

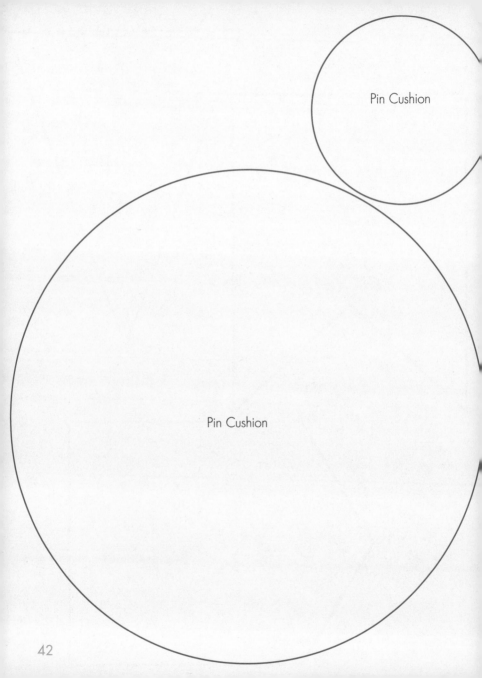

Pin Cushion

Pin Cushion

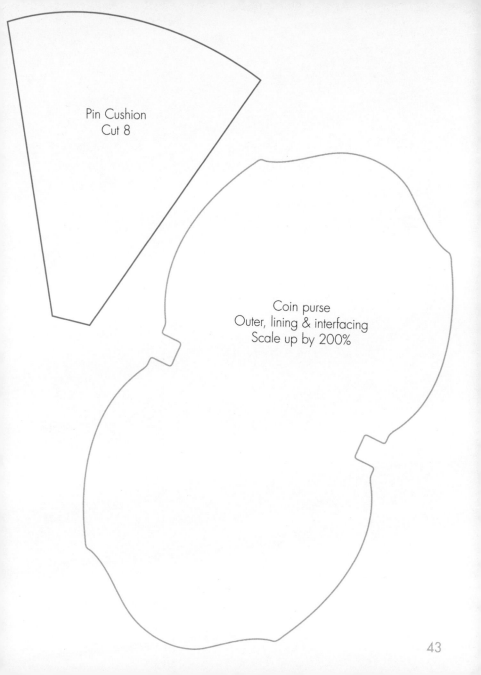

Pin Cushion
Cut 8

Coin purse
Outer, lining & interfacing
Scale up by 200%

Needle wrap
Small pocket lining
Scale up by 500%

Needle wrap
Small pocket front
Scale up by 500%

Needle wrap
Outside & inner
Scale up by 500%

Needle wrap
Top flap
Scale up by 500%

Needle wrap
Large pocket lining
Scale up by 500%

Needle wrap
Large pocket front
Scale up by 500%

Apron - Tie - Scale up by 1000%

Apron
Main
Scale up by 1000%

Apron
Pocket
Scale up by 1000%

Sewing caddy
Basket pieces (outer & lining)
Scale up by 500%

Sewing caddy
Pocket pieces (outer & lining)
Scale up by 500%

Author
Avec UK

Published by
Avec UK

DESIGNED IN
DORSET

Produced responsibly in China
Manufactured by Avec UK, BH22 9BU.
www.avecuk.com
For personal use only.
Not for resale

AVEC Trade Ltd. Second Edition
ISBN 9781916396760